YESHIVA
OF THE
TELSHE ALUMNI

The Yeshiva of the Telshe Alumni
Torah's Way Station in Riverdale

It is one of the oldest and, at the same time, one of the youngest institutions of higher Torah learning in the world. Established in the Riverdale community on the outskirts of New York City, a short distance from the major Jewish population centers of the New York metropolitan area, the Yeshiva of the Telshe Alumni is one of the youngest, most vibrant *yeshivos* in the world, with a venerable tradition going back over one hundred years.

The original Telshe Yeshiva was founded in 1875 in the small Lithuanian town of Telshe by Rabbi Eliezer Gordon. It was a time of great advances in Torah study brought on by the blossoming of the *yeshiva* movement, and within a short time, the Telshe Yeshiva took its place at the forefront of the great *yeshivos* of the period. Because of its rigid standards of academic excellence and the expert guidance and tutelage of its illustrious *roshei yeshiva*, many thousands of students from all over Europe, as well as a number of students from faraway America, flocked to the Telshe Yeshiva to develop as Torah scholars. After years of study, they would return to their native communities as leaders and exemplary figures, carrying the Telshe tradition to the far corners of the Jewish world.

In 1941, Nazi troops entered the town of Telshe and killed most of the faculty and student body in the *yeshiva*, but the small remnant that survived, under the leadership of Rabbi Eli Meir Bloch and Rabbi Chaim Mordechai Katz, reestablished the *yeshiva* with a handful of students in Cleveland, Ohio, in the fall of 1941. The new *yeshiva* became a rallying point for surviving students and alumni, and over the next two decades, th⸺⸺⸺⸺se to world prominence as a promi⸺⸺⸺ah learning and one of the most i⸺⸺⸺*iva* movement in America.

Although countless students f⸺⸺⸺ed

the Telshe *yeshivos* over the years, it was not until 1980 that the Yeshiva of the Telshe Alumni was established within the New York metropolitan area. The *yeshiva* is called the Yeshiva of the Telshe Alumni, because it was inspired and created by a founding committee of dedicated Telshe graduates who appreciated the importance of bringing the singular style and standards of Telshe scholarship to a wider public. After a brief stay in Westwood, New Jersey, the *yeshiva* relocated to a spacious, two-acre campus in Riverdale, New York, and its story is one of the great success stories of our times.

The Yeshiva of the Telshe Alumni has become one of the very finest institutions of its kind. The quality of the education is outstanding, rivalled only by the superb personal development engendered by the devoted faculty. As the *yeshiva* steadily grows in reputation and prestige, applications far exceed the capacity of the *yeshiva*, so that today the student body represents the flower of our Jewish youth, young men of exceptional talent and character who are being groomed to take their place among the leaders of the next generation. In the Yeshiva of the Telshe Alumni one can already catch a glimpse of the future of the Jewish people, and indeed, the future is bright.

Come see for yourself.

You'll be greeted and made welcome by the students. They'll bring you a chair, offer you a *siddur*, ask how they can help. You'll see a staff of profound, dedicated *Roshei Yeshiva* who represent the finest products of American and Israeli *yeshivos*. You'll see these educators guiding their students from early in the morning until late—very late—at night. You'll see classes that are not permitted to grow to a size that would inhibit this personal relationship. You'll see groups of physicians or professionals and business people from the community coming for their regular *shiur* in the Yeshiva. You'll see the cleanliness and order, and you'll feel the sense of mission that permeates the entire institution.

Seldom are expectations so well rewarded. That is why your much-needed suppport of YTA will accomplish so much.

לע״נ

האשה צפרה

בת **ר׳ צבי הכהן** ע״ה

ת.נ.צ.ב.ה.

MENORAS HAMAOR

The Jewish Child

RABBEINU YITZCHAK ABOHAV

Translated by
RABBI YAAKOV YOSEF REINMAN

CIS
P·U·B·L·I·S·H·E·R·S
New York · London · Jerusalem

ISBN 1-56062-059-5

Published and distributed
in the U.S., Canada and overseas by
C.I.S. Publishers and Distributors
180 Park Avenue, Lakewood, New Jersey 08701
(201) 905-3000 Fax: (201) 367-6666

Published in conjuction with
Yeshiva of the Telshe Alumni
4904 Independence Avenue
Riverdale, New York 10471

Distributed in Israel by
C.I.S. International (Israel)
Rechov Mishkalov 18
Har Nof, Jerusalem
Tel: 02-538-935

Distributed in the U.K. and Europe by
C.I.S. International (U.K.)
1 Palm Court, Queen Elizabeth Walk
London, England N16
Tel: 01-809-3723

Cover design by Deenee Cohen

PRINTED IN THE UNITED STATES OF AMERICA

Table of Contents

Translator's Foreword

Rabbeinu Yitzchak Abohav, the author of *Menoras Hamaor*, lived in Spain in the latter half of the fourteenth century. Spain, at that time, was the glittering diamond of the European continent. It enjoyed unparalleled prosperity. The lingering influence of the Moorish occupation made it a center of enlightenment. Philosophy and science, poetry and art flourished as nowhere else.

The Jews of Spain found this environment very hospitable, and indeed, it was there that they achieved their highest social station since being exiled from their homeland. Through their talent and industry, the Jewish people achieved the status of a privileged class, below the nobility but above the rest of the Spanish populace. Jews became the merchants and the financiers, the doctors and the poets, the philosophers and the ministers of the royal court; they became the "technocrats" of Spanish society. But in the end, they were corrupted. They became intoxicated by their unaccustomed social and economic freedom. They neglected the study of the Torah and the meticulous ovservance of *mitzvos*.

Perturbed by this corruption, Rabbeinu Yitzchak Abohav appealed to his people to rediscover the sweet taste of the Torah and "seek provision for their long journey into eternity." To accomplish this, he wrote a masterwork that encapsulated the basic elements of Judaism in a deceptively simple form, the classic *Menoras Hamaor*.

In the long run, *Menoras Hamaor* struck a responsive chord among the Jewish people. It filled the very real need for a concise

9

framework for the basic tenets of Judaism. *Menoras Hamaor* is an "easy read" that quotes the Agada without extensive comment, relying on it to be effective on an emotional level rather than an intellectual level. As such, it became one of the most beloved and widely read works of popular inspiration in Jewish religious literature. Not counting excerpts and synopses, it has appeared in seventy-six editions, originating in many cities across the European continent, North Africa, and the Near East.

This volume, *The Jewish Child*, is excerpted from *The Light of Mitzvos*. It deals with the obligations of child to parent and parent to child, focusing on the *mitzvos* of *kibud av va'eim*, honoring parents, and *chinuch*, bringing up children. Together, these two *mitzvos* form the foundation of the Jewish family.

Chapter One

THE THREE PARTNERS

Our sages expressed the greatness of the mitzvah of honoring parents by describing them as partners with the Holy Blessed One in the creation of the child. The Talmud tells us (Niddah 31a; Kedushin 30b):

> Our rabbis have taught: There are three partners in the creation of a person — his father, his mother, and the Holy Blessed One. The father produces the albumen from which the bones, the veins, the nails, the brain, and the white of the eye are formed. The mother produces the red matter from which the skin, the flesh, the blood, and the pupil of the eye are formed. And the Holy Blessed One instills in him a spirit, a soul, facial features, sight, hearing, speech, the ability to walk, intelligence, understanding, and wisdom. When the time comes for a person to depart from this world the Holy Blessed One takes away his part and leaves the parts of the father and the mother.
>
> Rav Pappa said: "This coincides with the popular saying that if you take away the salt you might as well throw the meat to the dogs."

11

Our rabbis have taught: It is written, Honor your father and your mother (Shemos 20:12), and it is written, Honor God with your wealth (Mishlei 3:9). The Scripture compares the honor of one's father and mother to the honor of the Holy Blessed One.

It is also written, Each man shall fear his mother and his father (Vayikra 19:3), and it is written, You shall fear God, your Lord (Devarim 6:13). The Scripture compares fear of one's father and mother to the fear of the Omnipresent One.

It is written, And he who curses his father and his mother... (Shemos 21:17), and it is written, A man who shall curse his Lord... (Vayikra 24:15). The Scripture compares "blessing" a father and mother to "blessing" the Omnipresent One.[1]

As to the prohibition against striking parents there can, of course, be no comparison there. The other comparisons, however, are only logical, since all three of them are partners in a person.

...Our rabbis have taught: There are three partners in the creation of a person — his father, his mother, and the Holy Blessed One.

The Holy Blessed One said: "As long as a person honors his father and mother I consider it as if I dwelled among them and they honored Me."

It was taught: It is perfectly clear before the One by whose Word the world was created that a child honors his mother more than his father because she appeases him with soft words. Therefore, the Scripture mentions the father before the mother in the mitzvah of honoring parents. It is perfectly clear before the One by whose Word the world was created that a child fears his father more than his mother because his father teaches him Torah. Therefore, the Scripture mentions the mother before the father in the mitzvah of fearing parents.

The Talmud also tell us (Yerushalmi, Kedushin 1:7):

Rabbi Shimeon the son of Yochai taught: "So great is the honor

---

1. [Translator's note: A common Talmudic euphemism.]

of a father and a mother that the Holy Blessed One gave it more importance than His own honor. For it is written, Honor God with your wealth (Mishlei 3:9), a reference to the leket, shikcha, pe'ah, terumah, and maaser portions of the harvest. If you have a harvest from which to give these portions you are obliged to do so, but if you do not you have no obligation. As to parents, however, it is written, Honor your father and your mother (Shemos 20:12), with no qualifications. You are obliged to do so whether or not you have the means, even if it means collecting from door to door."

Chapter Two

THE COMMANDMENT AND ITS REWARD

Honor your father and your mother (Shemos 20:12) is the fifth of the Ten Commandments. The first four commandments deal with the relationship of a person to the Blessed One Himself and His Honor, the fifth is to honor parents, and the last five are ethical instructions for personal conduct.

It has been said that the first five commandments were on one tablet, and the last five commandments on another.[2] It has been further suggested[3] that the first five represent the Written Law, while the last five represent the Oral Law. The Midrash tells us that the two Tablets represented the heavens and the earth, groom and bride, Moshe and Aharon, the two worlds (Tanchuma, Ki Sisa 16), all things deriving from one Source.

No matter what interpretation we put on the division of the Ten Commandments into two parts, the commandment of honoring parents is always connected to the first commandments which are for the honor of the Blessed Omnipresent One. Therefore, the sages stated that the honor of a father and a mother is compared to the honor of Hashem.[4]

---

2. This is also implied in *The Book of Creation* which tells us that the Ten Spheres (Kabbalistic Names) correspond to ten fingers, five facing five, with the Covenant in the center.

3. [Translator's note: Ramban, Shemos 20:12.]

We also find that it was this commandment that convinced the nations of the world to accept the first four commandments as well. The Talmud tells us (Kedushin 31a):

> *Rabbi Yehudah the Great expounded on the threshold of the Academy of the Prince: "What is the meaning of that which is written, All the kings of the earth shall acknowledge You, O God, for they have heard the Sayings of Your Mouth (Tehillim 138:4)? Why does the verse mention not just one Saying but many Sayings?*
>
> *"When the Holy Blessed One said: 'I am God your Lord' (Shemos 20:2) and, 'You shall have no other deities before Me' (Shemos 20:3), the nations of the world said: 'He has His own honor in mind.' But when He said: 'Honor your father and your mother' (Shemos 20:12), they acknowledged the truth of the first commandments as well."*
>
> *Rava said in the name of Rabbi Yitzchak: "This point can be inferred from that which is written, The beginning of Your Word is truth (Tehillim 119:160). Is not 'the end of Your Word' truth, too? Only, this is saying that just as 'the end of Your Word' is clearly truth so is 'the beginning of Your Word' truth as well."*

Furthermore, this is the only one of the Ten Commandments in which the Torah explicitly states the rewards for the fulfillment of the mitzvah, as it is written, Honor your father and your mother so that your life may be prolonged (Shemos 20:12), and it is also written, Honor your father and your mother so that your life may be prolonged and that it may be good for you (Devarim 5:16). The Talmud speaks of the fundamental nature of this reward (Bava Kama 54b; Chulin 142a, Kedushin 39b):

> *Rabbi Chanina the son of Agul asked Rabbi Chiya the son of Aba: "Why do the Ten Commandments on the first set of*

---

4. [Translator's note: See previous chapter.]

tablets not specify the reward 'that it may be good for you' as do those on the second set?"

He replied: *"...Go ask Rabbi Tanchum the son of Chanilai. He would often visit Rabbi Yehoshua the son of Levi who was familiar with the Agada."*

Rabbi Chanina the son of Agul went to Rabbi Tanchum the son of Chanilai and asked him.

He replied: *"I did not hear an answer to this question from Rabbi Yehoshua the son of Levi, but this is the answer of Rabbi Shmuel the son of Tanchum, the uncle of Rabbi Acha the son of Chanina, or according to another version, the grandfather of Rabbi Acha the son of Chanina: 'It is because the first Tablets were destined to be broken.'"*

How does the fact that they were destined to be broken answer the question?

Because if these words had been written on the first set when it was broken, it might have been an evil portent, Heaven forbid, that beneficience would cease from the Jewish people.

It was taught: Rabbi Eliezer the son of Yaakov says: *"There is no mitzvah in the Torah for which the reward is explicitly stated that is not connected with the ultimate resurrection of the dead.*

"In reference to the mitzvah of honoring parents it is written, Honor your father and your mother so that your life may be prolonged and that it may be good for you (Devarim 5:16). And in reference to the mitzvah of sending away the mother bird when taking the young from a bird's nest it is written, If a bird's nest appears before you on the way...you shall not take the mother along with the young, surely shall you send away the mother, and the young you can take for yourself so that it may be good for you, and your life may be prolonged (Devarim 22:6-7).

"What if someone's father told him: 'Climb up on the roof and bring me the fledglings that are nested there,' then he climbed up, sent off the mother and took the fledglings, and on

his way down he fell and died? Where is the goodness and
longevity for this person? Only, 'that it may be good for you'
means that you will inherit a world that is totally good, and
'that your life may be prolonged' means that you will inherit a
world that is eternally long."

What is the basis for this question? How do we know that
something like this would happen?

Rabbi Yaakov said: "Such an incident actually happened."

Maybe, as he was climbing down from the roof, the person
was thinking about committing a sin and was therefore
punished. If so, what does this incident prove?

The Holy Blessed One does not view mere evil intentions as
if they had resulted in acts.[5]

Still, maybe he had idolatrous thoughts at the time he was
climbing down from the roof. For it is written, In order to
grasp the House of Yisrael by their heart (Yechezkel 14:5),
and Rav Acha the son of Yaakov said: "This refers to
idolatrous thoughts."

Rabbi Eliezer the son of Yaakov does not exclude this
possibility. Only, he says, if the reward for these mitzvos were
intended for this world, surely they would have shielded him
from his sinful thoughts.

Still, how could such an incident have taken place? Did not
Rabbi Elazar say: "People on a mission of mitzvah are
protected from injury"?

That is referring to someone on the way to do a mitzvah.

But did not Rabbi Elazar say: "People on a mission of
mitzvah are protected from injury, both on the way there and
on the way back"?

Indeed, but the incident involved a rickety ladder on which
injury was likely. And where injury is likely one should not
expect a miracle, as it is written, And Shmuel said, How can I

---

5. [Translator's note: This is a privilege exclusive to the Jewish people. See
Tosefos.]

go? for Shaul will hear of it, and he will kill me, and God said, take a calf in your hand and say, I have come to sacrifice to God (Shmuel II 16:2).

Rav Yosef said: "If only Acher[6] had interpreted these verses as did his nephew Rabbi Yaakov he would not have sinned."

What did he see?

Some say he saw an incident similar to the one Rabbi Yaakov had seen.

Others say that he saw the severed tongue of a great man[7] being dragged about by a swine and said: "How can it be that a mouth that gave forth such pearls should now lick the dust!?"

---

6. [Translator's note: Literally, "that other one" or "the outsider", this is the way the Talmud refers to Elisha the son of Avuya, a great Tanna who fell into bad ways. Tosefos, in Chagigah 15a, quotes a Yerushalmi in which Acher himself reveals the reason for his eventual downfall. When Acher was born, his father Avuya, who was himself an aristocratic member of Yerushalayim's high society, invited all the other members of the aristocracy to the bris milah (circumcision ceremony). He also invited Rabbi Eliezer and Rabbi Yehoshua and seated them in a separate room. All the noblemen were busy with what interested them, drinking and dancing. Rabbi Eliezer and Rabbi Yehoshua decided to busy themselves with what interested them, learning the Torah. As they sat there absorbed in the Torah a fire descended from Heaven and surrounded them. Avuya asked them: "Have you come to my house to burn it down?" They replied: "Heaven forbid! We were sitting and studying the Torah, and its words were as delightful as when it was first given on Mount Sinai. Was it not given then amidst a fire?" Avuya was impressed. He said: "If this is the power of Torah then if this infant we are circumcizing today survives I am dedicating his life to the Torah." Since Avuya's motivation was for glory rather than the sake of Heaven he was deemed unworthy, and his son eventually fell into bad ways.]

7. [Translator's note: In the standard text this great man is identified as Chutzpis the Meturgeman. Tosefos, in Chagigah 15a, quotes a Yerushalmi that identifies this man as Rabbi Yehudah the Nachtom.]

Chapter Three

HOW TO HONOR A PARENT

The Talmud tells us what the mitzvah of honoring parents entails (Kedushin 31b; 32a):

> Our rabbis have taught: One must honor him when he is alive, and one must honor him after he dies.
>
> How does a person honor his living father?
>
> If he knows that the people of this place respect his father as much as they respect him he should not say: "Send me for my sake," or "Hurry for my sake." Rather, whatever he requests should be for his father's sake.[8]
>
> How does a person honor his departed father?
>
> When he repeats something that his father once said he should not say merely: "This is what my father said." Rather, he should say: "This what my father, my master, said." And he should add: "May I be the atonement for his resting place."
>
> However, this last phrase should only be said during the first twelve months after the father's death. Afterwards, he should say: "May he be remembered for the eternal life of the world to come."[9]

---

8. [Translator's note: Unless his own standing is greater in this place and a request for his own sake would be more effective. (Rashi)]

9. [Translator's note: Rashi explains that the phrase "May I be the atonement for

Our Rabbis have taught: When a Torah scholar is expounding the Torah and repeats something that his father or teacher had taught him he must not utter the name of his father or his teacher. However, the meturgeman[10] need not avoid uttering the name of his father or his teacher.

Whose father? The meturgeman's? Is not he too obliged to respect his father?

Rabah the son of Rav Huna said: "The meturgeman need not avoid uttering the name of the Torah scholar's father or teacher."

Such was the case with Mar the son of Rav Ashi. When he would expound he would say: "So said my father, my master." And the Amora who served as meturgeman would say: "So said Rav Ashi."

Our rabbis have taught: What sort of things come under the heading of fearing a parent and what sort of things come under the heading of honoring a parent?

Fearing a parent means not standing or sitting in his regular place, not contradicting him, and not offering an opinion on a Halachic issue that is at variance with his father's opinion. Honoring a parent means feeding him, giving him to drink, clothing him, covering him, escorting him in, and escorting him out.

At whose expense?

Rav Yehudah said: "At the son's expense."

Rav Nassan the son of Oshia said: "At the father's expense."

The rabbis sent a ruling to Rav Yehudah, or according to another version, to Rav Yirmiyah, that it is at the father's expense. And this is the authoritative ruling.

It was taught: If a person's father is violating the Torah he

---

his resting place" is an expression of the son's willingness to accept on himself the retribution in store for the father. Punishment for Jewish people, however, is limited to a maximum of twelve months (Rosh Hashanah 16b).]

10.[Translator's note: This Aramaic word normally translates to "interpreter" or "translator". However, in this particular usage the reference is to a "circulator" who, upon occasion of large assemblages, used to relay the teachings of the rabbi to the people who were out of earshot. See Rashi in Pesachim 50b).]

should not tell him: "Father, you have violated the words of the Torah." Rather, he should say: "This is what is written in the Torah, and this is what is written in the Torah."

But will not such a specific statement of what is permitted and what is not permitted also cause his father pain?

Only, this is what he should say: "Father, this is one of the verses that is written in the Torah."

The Talmud also tells us the limits of the mitzvah of honoring parents (Bava Metzia 32a; Kedushin 32a):

Our rabbis have taught: I might have thought that a person should obey his father even if he tells him to contaminate himself (if he is a kohen) or not to return a lost object that he has found. Therefore, it is written, Each man shall fear his mother and his father, and you shall observe my sabbaths (Vayikra 19:3), the inference being that all of you are obliged to honor Me.

Can it be that if it were not for the juxtaposition of these two mitzvos in the same verse we might have thought that a person should obey his father even where it involves a sin? Why should this be so? Failure to return a lost object, or contamination by a kohen, violates both a positive commandment and a prohibition, and a positive commandment, such as honoring parents, cannot override the combination of a positive commandment and a prohibition.

I might have thought that since the honor of parents is compared to the honor of the Omnipresent, as is apparent from the juxtaposition of that which is written, Honor God with your wealth (Mishlei 3:9) and that which is written, Honor your father and your mother (Shemos 20:12), one should obey parents in all circumstances. Therefore, this special derivation was needed to teach us otherwise.

Rabbi Elazar the son of Masia says: "If my father would tell me: 'Give me a drink of water' at the time that I have a mitzvah to perform I would disregard the honor of my father and perform the mitzvah. For both I and my father are obliged to perform mitzvos."

> *Isi the son of Yehudah says: "If it is possible for this mitzvah to be performed by someone else let that other person do it and let he himself attend to the honor of his father."*
>
> *Rav Acha the son of Masna said: "The authoritative ruling endorses the opinion of Isi the son of Yehudah."*

Although we have seen that the honor of parents is compared to the honor of the Omnipresent, a Torah teacher always takes precedence over a father, unless the father is himself a Torah scholar. The Talmud tells us (Bava Metzia 33a):

> *If a person has the opportunity of salvaging either the lost object of his father or the lost object of his Torah teacher the lost object of his Torah teacher takes precedence over the lost object of his father. For his father provides with life in this world while his Torah teacher, who taught him Torah and wisdom, provides him with life both in this world and in the world to come. But if his father is a Torah scholar on a level with his teacher the lost object of his father takes precedence.[11]*
>
> *If his father and his teacher are both carrying heavy burdens he should first help his teacher unload his burden and then help his father.*
>
> *If both his father and his teacher are in captivity he should first ransom his teacher and then his father. But if his father is a Torah scholar he should first ransom his father and then his teacher.*

---

11. [Translator's note: It is assumed that in this case the father is also his teacher to some extent.]

Chapter Four

EXAMPLES FROM THE TALMUD

It would be fitting for the Jewish people, who received the Torah and were given the mitzvah of honoring parents among the Ten Commandments, to learn from the example of some gentiles who were not given this mitzvah and nevertheless fulfilled it on a very high level. The Talmud tells us (Kedushin 31a):

It was asked of Rav Ula the Great: "How far is the extent of the mitzvah of honoring parents?"

He replied: "Take a look at what a gentile named Dama the son of Nesinah did for his father in Ashkelon. Once, the sages came to Dama the son of Nesinah to buy precious stones for the urim vetumim on the breastplate of the ephod vestment of the kohen gadol, and they were prepared to pay six hundred thousand coins for it. And according to Rav Kehana it was a million coins. Nesinah was sleeping at the time, and the key to the storeroom was under his pillow. Dama refused to disturb his father.

"The following year, Dama the son of Nesinah received his reward. A red heifer was born among his herd. The sages of the Jewish people came to him to buy the heifer to use as a parah adumah for the purification of the contaminated.

"Dama the son of Nesinah told them: 'I know full well that if I

would ask you for all the money in the world that you are prepared to give it to me. However, all I ask of you is the money I lost last year out of respect for my father.'

"When the sages heard this they marvelled: 'If someone who has not been commanded to fulfill the mitzvah does this, certainly someone who has been commanded to fulfill the mitzvah must do even more.'

"As Rabbi Chanina said: 'One who does because he is commanded is greater than one who does even though he has not been commanded.'"

Rav Yosef said: "At first I used to say that if someone would tell me that the authoritative ruling endorses the opinion of Rabbi Yehudah that blind people are not obliged to fulfill the mitzvos I would make a feast for the rabbis. I thought that it was to my merit that I fulfilled the mitzvos even though I was not commanded to do so. But now that I have heard the teaching of Rabbi Chanina that the fulfillment of one who is commanded to do is greater than the fulfillment of one who is not commanded to do I would make a feast for the rabbis if someone told me that the authoritative ruling is against Rabbi Yehudah's opinion."

When Rav Dimi came from Eretz Yisrael he said: "Once, Dama the son of Nesinah was wearing a garment woven of gold thread and sitting among the Roman noblemen. His mother came in, ripped the garment from him, hit him on the head with it, and spit in his face, and still, he did nothing to humiliate her."

It was asked of Rabbi Eliezer: "How far is the extent of the mitzvah of honoring parents?"

He replied: "Even if a father takes his son's purse and tosses it into the sea the son must do nothing to humiliate the father."

Elsewhere, the Talmud tells of how our sages honored their parents with kindness to the best of their abilities (Kedushin 31a):

Avimi the son of Rabbi Abahu taught: "It is possible for someone to feed his parents exotic poultry and through this to lose his share in the world to come. It is also possible for someone to put his father to work on a millstone and through this to gain everlasting life in the world to come. All depends on how it is done."12

Rabbi Abahu said: "Just as my son Avimi fulfills the mitzvah of honoring parents."

Avimi had five ordained sons, but when his father would appear on the doorstep Avimi himself would run to open the door, calling out: "Yes, yes, I'm coming" until he reached the door.

One day, Rabbi Abahu said to Avimi: "Give me a drink of water."

In the short time it took Avimi to bring the water Rabbi Abahu fell asleep. Avimi leaned over and waited until his father awakened. While he was waiting the explanation of one of the psalms he had never understood suddenly became clear to him.

Rabbi Yaakov the son of Aba said to Abaye: "What should I do if, when I come home from the academy, my father has poured me a cup and my mother has also prepared some wine for me?"

He replied: "Take from your mother, not from your father. Since he is a Torah scholar it is demeaning for him to serve you."

Rabbi Tarfon had an old mother. Whenever she had to go to bed he would bend over, and she would use his back to step up onto her bed. He told his colleagues in the study hall about what he was doing.

They said to him: "You have not even reached the halfway point in the fulfillment of the mitzvah of honoring parents. Has she tossed away your purse in front of you and you did nothing to humiliate her?"

Whenever Rav Yosef would hear his mother's footsteps approaching he would say: "I must stand up in honor of the Divine

---

12.[Translator's note: Tosefos brings two illustrations from the Yerushalmi. It once happened that a son gave his father exotic poultry to eat. His father asked him: "From where do you get such things?" He replied: "Why do you need to know, old man, as long as you are chomping and eating?" It also happened that a man used to mill grain with a millstone. He had an old father who was conscripted to work as a miller in the service of the king. The son said: "You work the millstone in my stead, and I will go take your place in the service of the king. Any humiliation you would suffer I will suffer. Any lashes you would receive I will receive."]

Presence that approaches."[13]

Rabbi Yochanan said: "Fortunate is the person that has never known his parents."[14]

Rabbi Yochanan's father died right after he was conceived, and his mother died right after he was born. This was also the case with Abaye.

But did not Abaye always say: "My mother told me"?

That was his nursemaid.

Rav Isi had an old mother.

She said to him: "I want jewelry."

He got it for her.

She said: "I want a husband."

He said: "I will search for someone for you."

She said: "I want someone as handsome as you."

In frustration, he left her behind and went to Eretz Yisrael. When he arrived he heard that his mother was coming to join him.

He asked Rabbi Yochanan: "Is it permitted to go out of Eretz Yisrael?"

Rabbi Yochanan replied: "It is forbidden."

He asked: "What if it is to welcome one's mother?"

Rabbi Yochanan replied: "I don't know," and he became a little angry.

Isi then came back to ask Rabbi Yochanan once again if he is permitted to go out.

Rabbi Yochanan said: "Isi, you have decided to leave. May the Omnipresent return you home in peace."

Isi came before Rabbi Elazar, told him what happened, and asked him: "Is it possible, Heaven forbid, that Rabbi Yochanan is angry at me?"

---

13. [Translator's note: Maharsha explains that this is according to that which the Talmud tells us (Kedushin 30b): The Holy Blessed One said: "As long as a person honors his father and mother I consider it as if I dwelled among them and they honored Me." See Chapter One.]

14. [Translator's note: Rashi explains that Rabbi Yochanan is of the opinion that this is such a difficult mitzvah to fulfill that it is almost impossible not to violate it and bring retribution upon one's head.]

Rabbi Elazar asked: "What did he say to you?"

Isi replied: "May the Omnipresent return you home in peace."

Rabbi Elazar said: "If he had been angry at you he would not have blessed you."

As Isi was leaving he heard that it was his mother's coffin that was being brought to Eretz Yisrael.

He said: "If I had known I would not have left."

Chapter Five

THE IMPORTANCE OF CONTINUITY

The Torah emphasizes the importance of being fruitful and multiplying, repeating this commandment four times (Beraishis 1:28; Ibid. 9:1; Ibid. 9:7; Ibid. 35:11). The Talmud tells us that this mitzvah is not considered fulfilled until one has both a male and a female child (Yevamos 61b). The Talmud also tells us that the mitzvah of being fruitful and multiplying is considered fulfilled only so long as one's children survive (Ibid. 62a). Thus, the fulfillment of this mitzvah is a long, ongoing process that begins with the birth of the child, continues with the upbringing of the child, and is completed only with the assured continuation of one's lineage through the birth of grandchildren.

Elsewhere, the Talmud discusses the importance of continuity, especially the continuity provided by a male heir (Bava Basra 116a):

> Rabbi Yochanan said in the name of Rabbi Shimeon the son of Yochai: "The Holy Blessed One is full of wrath at those that neglect to leave male heirs..."
>
> It is written, Those that are oblivious of mortality and do not fear the Lord (Tehillim 55:20). There is a difference of opinion between Rabbi Yochanan and Rabbi Yehoshua the son of Levi as to the meaning of this verse.

One says: "This refers to anyone that does not leave a son behind him."

The other says: "This refers to anyone that does not leave a disciple behind him."

...Rabbi Pinchas the son of Chama expounded: "What is the meaning of that which is written, And Hadad heard in Mitzraim that David had gone to rest with his forefathers and that Yoav the general of the army had died (Melachim I 11:21)? Why does the verse refer to David as having gone to rest and to Yoav as having died?

"David who had left a son behind him is said to have gone to his rest, while Yoav who left no son behind him is said to have died."

How can it be said that Yoav left no son behind him? Is it not written, And from the sons of Yoav, Ovadiah the son of Yechiel (Ezra 8:9)?

Only, David who left behind him a son comparable to himself is said to have gone to his rest, while Yoav who did not leave behind him a son comparable to himself is said to have died.

Clearly, being fruitful and multiplying entails more than giving birth to children and seeing to their physical survival. It is also important to give them a proper upbringing, to condition them to follow the straight path, to prepare them for life. The Talmud elaborates (Kedushin 29a):

Our Rabbis have taught: A person's obligations to his son include circumcizing him, ritual redemption if he is a firstborn, teaching him Torah, finding him a wife, and teaching him a skill.

Others say: "Teaching him to swim in a river as well."

Rabbi Yehudah says: "Whoever does not teach his son a skill has taught him thievery."

How can it be said that he has taught him thievery?

Only, it is as if he has encouraged him to engage in thievery.

...To what extent is a person required to teach his son Torah?

Rav Yehudah said in the name of Shmuel: "An example can be taken from Zevulun the son of Dan whose grandfather taught him

Scripture, Mishnah, Talmud, Halachah, and Agadah."

...Why was his grandfather required to teach him Torah? Have we not been taught otherwise?

For it was taught: It is written, And you shall teach them to your sons (Devarim 11:19), the inference apparently being that you are not required to teach Torah to your grandsons.

What then is the meaning of that which is written, And you shall make them known to your sons and to the sons of your sons (Ibid. 4:9)?

This verse comes to teach us that whoever teaches Torah to his sons is considered to have taught it to all of his offspring in all future generations.

The grandfather of Zevulun the son of Dan follows the alternative interpretation contained in that which has been taught: It is written, And you shall teach them to your sons (Devarim 11:19). This would seem to refer only to sons. How do we know to include grandsons as well? For it is written, And you shall make them known to your sons and to the sons of your sons (Ibid. 4:9). Why does the other verse mention sons? It is meant to teach that one is required to teach Torah to one's sons, not to one's daughters.

The Talmud tells us that the best skill that a person can teach his son is the study of Torah, for it will provide for him in this world and sustain him in the world to come (Kedushin 82a):

Rabbi Nehorai said to them: "I would put aside all other skills in the world and only teach my sons the Torah, for they would then be able to enjoy the reward of their toil in this world and its substance would endure for them in the world to come.

"For all the skills in the world are only useful to a person in his youth and when he has his strength. If he falls ill, however, or if he is afflicted by suffering, or when he becomes old, he can no longer maintain his profession. He could very well die of starvation. Not so with the Torah. It helps him develop and protects him in his youth, and it provides a future and hope in his old age.

"Moreover, the Blessed Omnipresent One loves righteous people

in their old age more than in their youth."[15]

What is it written of the young?

It is written, And those that yearn for God shall find renewed strength, they shall spread out their wings like eagles (Yeshayahu 40:31).

What is it written of the old?

It is written, Even more shall they flourish in their old age (Tehillim 92:15).[16]

And so do we find that our forefather Avraham fulfilled the entire Torah before it was even given, as it is written, Because Avraham heeded My Voice (Beraishis 26:5), the Hebrew word used here for "because" also meaning "before" in an alternate usage, and the Holy Blessed One blessed him more in his youth than in his old age.

What was the blessing Avraham received in his youth?

It is written, And I shall establish you as a great nation (Beraishis 12:2).

What was the blessing that Avraham received in his old age?

It is written, And Avraham grew old, full of days, and God blessed him with everything (Beraishis 24:1).

---

15. [Translator's note: This statement does not appear in the standard text. According to the author's version the subsequent quotes are intended to prove that the rewards of old age are greater than the rewards of youth.]

16. [Translator's note: The Hebrew phrase used here is *od yenuvun b'sayvah.* Ordinarily, this would be translated as "still shall they flourish". However, according to the author's version of the text, the intent is to prove that the rewards of old age are greater than the rewards of youth (see Footnote 15). Therefore, the alternate translation used here is indicated.]

Chapter Six

HOW TO TEACH THE TORAH

$\mathbf{A}$ person should always make every effort to teach his son Torah during the childhood years, taking into consideration the child's stamina and age in determining how much of the yoke of Torah the child can bear.

How should one do this?

When the child learns to speak the parent should teach him some verses from the Torah.[17] Among the verses often used are that which is written, The Torah which Moshe commanded us is the heritage of the community of Yaakov (Devarim 33:4), and that which is written, Hear Yisrael, God is our Lord, God is One (Devarim 6:4). The purpose of beginning this early is to consecrate part of the early gift of speech to the service of Hashem.

The parent must try to make the learning of Torah a pleasant experience for the child. He must see what the child likes and desires and use these things to reward the child for his studies. In this way the child will be conditioned to study willingly.

As the child grows older and no longer cares for the little rewards of his younger years the parent should reward him according to his current tastes. When the child outgrows material rewards the parent should point out other compensations for learning the Torah. He should tell the child: "Learn Torah so that you will be seated in the

---

17. [Translator's note: According to Sukkah 42a.]

place of honor, you will be called rabbi, and you will be treated with respect." When this no longer impresses the child the parent should say: "Learn Torah so that you will earn a place in the Garden of Eden."

Ultimately, if the child is conditioned to study the Torah, he will come to perceive the truth that lies within it. He will learn to enjoy the study of the Torah. He will develop a love for the Torah and study it for its own sake.

The Talmud tells us that a parent should not press a child to study before the age of six or seven, other than a small amount through coaxing (Bava Basra 21a):

> Rav Yehudah said in the name of Rav: "The man named Yehoshua the son of Gamla must be remembered fondly indeed, because if it were not for him the Jewish people would have forgotten the Torah.
>
> "At first, whoever had a father was taught Torah by his own father, and whoever had no father could not study the Torah. How do we know this? For it is written, And you shall teach them to your sons (Devarim 11:19). Therefore, it was instituted that there would be teachers in Yerushalayim. But still, whoever had a father was taken by his father to Yerushalayim where he could be taught the Torah, and whoever had no father could not go to Yerushalayim to study. Therefore, it was instituted that there should be teachers in every region. Students would come in at the age of sixteen or seventeen, and if the teacher would get angry at a student he would expel him. Finally, Yehoshua the son of Gamla instituted that there be teachers in every province and every town and that the children be brought to them at the age of six or seven."
>
> Rav said to Rav Shmuel the son of Sheylas: "Do not accept a child below the age of six, but from that age and above accept them and imbue them with the Torah as you would feed a hungry ox."
>
> And Rav also said to Rav Shmuel the son of Sheylas: "When you strike a child use only something harmless such as

a sandal thong. If the child begins to learn all is well. If he doesn't respond, however, do not continue to strike him. Instead, try to pair him with a more diligent study partner."

Elsewhere, the Talmud tells us (Kesubos 50a):

Rabbi Yitzchak said: "It was instituted at the synod in Usha that a parent should be very patient with a child who refuses to learn. If the child reaches the age of twelve and still refuses to learn the parent should use strong disciplinary measures."

Did we not learn otherwise? Did not Rav say to Rav Shmuel the son of Sheylas: "Do not accept children below the age of six, but from that age and above accept them and imbue them with the Torah as you would feed a hungry ox"?

There is no contradiction. The age of six is when he begins to study Scripture, the age of twelve when he begins to study the Mishnah. As indeed Abaye has said: "My nursemaid[18] told me: 'Scripture at age six, Mishnah at age seven, fasting from beginning to end on fast days at age thirteen or at age twelve for girls.'"

...Rav said: "Whoever brings his son to study Torah before the age of six will find his efforts to sustain the health of the child unsuccessful."

In another version: "The child's friends who are introduced to Torah study at a later age will find their attempts to catch up with him unsuccessful."

Although these versions seem to be contradictory, both are in fact valid. The first version, which looks askance at such practices, is referring to a weak child. The second version, which favors such practices, is referring to a strong child.

In fact, so great is the importance of teaching one's children Torah that we find the illustrious Chizkiah, King of Yehudah,

---

18. [Translator's note: Abaye often quotes from the wisdom of *aym*, the Hebrew word for mother. Elsewhere, however, the Talmud explains that Abaye's mother died during his early childhood and that these references are to Abaye's nursemaid (Kedushin 31b). See Chapter Four.]

carrying his children on his own shoulders to study the Torah (Berachos 10b).

However, teaching one's children Torah is in itself insufficient. It must be accompanied by a strong emphasis on fulfillment of the practical mitzvos. The Talmud outlines the proper method for conditioning one's children to fulfill the mitzvos (Sukkah 28a, Ibid. 42a; Yoma 82a):

> *A small child who no longer needs his mother's constant attention is required to sit in the sukkah. If a small child is capable of shaking the lulav correctly his father should buy him a lulav. A small child who knows how to dress himself is required to wear tsitsis.*

> *Rav Nachman said: "At age nine or ten a child should be conditioned to fast during fast days for a limited part of the day."*

The Talmud mentions only a few examples of conditioning children to do mitzvos, these examples being guidelines for determining when and how to go about conditioning children to fulfill *all* the mitzvos.

Shlomo Hamelech expressed the importance of conditioning during the youthful years when he wrote, Condition the youth according to his way, then even when he grows old it will not desert him (Mishlei 22:6). This verse clearly expresses the lasting effects of early conditioning. The exact intent, however, is subject to interpretation.

According to one approach, the verse is referring to positive parental conditioning. It is telling us to condition our children during the years of their youth to study the Torah, perform the mitzvos, and conduct themselves ethically. Once it becomes second nature to them they will certainly continue to do so in their old age, especially since people are less affected by physical temptation in their old age.

This verse can also be interpreted as referring to the negative results of the lack of parental conditioning. In this sense, it would be telling us that if a child is permitted to follow the dictates of his nature, to idle away his time and let himself be ruled by his evil inclination, then he will not be able to break out of this pattern even in his old age. It will have become too deeply ingrained in his nature.

According to the second interpretation, this verse is similar to that which is written, Revel, O young man, in your youth...but know that for all these things the Lord will bring you to judgment (Koheles 11:9). That verse tells us that if one passes his youth in revelry he will ultimately be brought to judgment before Hashem. This verse tells us that if one lets a youth become accustomed to yielding to his inclinations he will not change when he grows older, but if you condition him to do mitzvos he will become greater as he grows older.

Chapter Seven

MOLDING A CHILD

Although a parent should always treat his child with love, that love must never prevent the parent from disciplining the child. On the contrary, the failure to discipline a child when the situation demands it reflects a lack of love and will ultimately cause the child to fall into bad ways. The Midrash tells us (Shemos Rabah 1:1):

> It is written, He who withholds his rod despises his son, but if he loves him he greets him with chastisement (Mishlei 13:24).
>
> In the way of the world, if a parent is told that someone hit his son he reacts violently. What then is the meaning of "he who withholds his rod despises his son"?
>
> It comes to teach you that if someone is reluctant to punish his child that child will ultimately fall into bad ways.
>
> We find this to be the case with Yishmael. Avraham was very devoted to him and did not punish him, and in the end, Yishmael fell into bad ways. Eventually, Avraham despised him and banished him emptyhanded from his home.
>
> What did Yishmael do?
>
> When Yishmael was fifteen years old he began bringing home images from outside and playing.[19] "Playing" refers to idolatry, as

---

19. [Translator's note: The Midrash is expanding upon that which is written, And Sarah saw that the son of Hagar the Egyptian, whom she had borne to Avraham, was playing (Beraishis 21:9).]

in that which is written, And they rose to play (Shemos 32:6). He would worship these idols in the manner he had seen others worship them. Sarah immediately reacted, as it is written, And she said to Avraham, Cast out this bondswoman and her son (Beraishis 21:10), her concern being that her son Yitzchak not be influenced by Yishmael's ways.

We find this to be the case with Yitzchak and his son Eisav as well, as is written, And Yitzchak loved Eisav (Beraishis 25:28). And because Yitzchak was reluctant to punish him Eisav fell into bad ways. The Talmud tells us (Bava Basra 16b):

Eisav committed five sins on that day. He cohabited with a betrothed maiden. He committed murder. He rejected the concept of the resurrection of the dead. He denied the existence of God. He disgraced his birthright as firstborn.

Furthermore, he yearned for the death of his father and attempted to kill his brother, as it is written, Let the days of mourning for my father draw near (Beraishis 27:41).

And he caused Yaakov to flee from the home of his fathers. Then Eisav himself left and went to Yishmael to learn from his bad ways in order to add more guilt to his sinfulness, as it is written, And Eisav went to Yishmael... (Beraishis 28:9).

Similarly, we find that David was reluctant to punish his son Avshalom, who consequently fell into bad ways. Avshalom eventually attempted to murder his father, cohabited with his father's wives and otherwise brought him endless grief and sorrow, and caused the deaths of thousands of Jewish people through his insurrection. The Talmud tells us (Berachos 7b):

Rabbi Shimeon the son of Yochai said: "Falling into bad ways is more destructive to a person's household than the War of Gog and Magog. For of Avshalom it is written, A song of David when he fled from his son Avshalom, O God, how numerous are my oppressors! my assailants are many (Tehillim 3:1-2), while of the

War of Gog and Magog it is written, Why do the nations rage and the peoples plan in vain? (Tehillim 2:1)."

Clearly, it is the responsibility of parents to train and mold their children, exerting discipline and authority and dispensing appropriate punishment whenever it is indicated. Only thus can parents prevent their children from falling into bad ways. The same applies to a teacher as regards the pupils who have been entrusted to him. If, however, the parent faithfully executes his responsibilities and is successful with all his children, or the teacher with all his disciples, it is considered a great merit. The Talmud tells us (Berachos 17a):

When the rabbis took their leave from the school of Rav Chisda they used to say to each other: "That our lords may bear their burdens, that there be no breach, nor emergence, nor outcry in our streets (Tehillim 144:14)."

What is the meaning of "that our lords may bear their burdens"?

There is a difference of opinion between Rav and Shmuel.

One says: "'Our lords' are those great in Torah, and 'their burdens' are the mitzvos."

The other says: "'Our lords' are those great in Torah and mitzvos, and 'their burdens' are their suffering."

What is the meaning of "that there be no breach"?

It is as if to say,"that our group should not be like Shaul's group of which Do'eg the Edomi was a member."

What is the meaning of "nor emergence"?

It is as if to say,"that our group should not be like David's group from which Achitofel emerged."

What is the meaning of "nor outcry"?

It is as if to say,"that our group should not be like Elisha's group from which Gaychazi emerged."[20]

---

20. [Translator's note: Tosefos explains that "outcry" applies to Gaychazi since Eliasha cursed him with leprosy (Melachim II 5:27) and a leper is required to call out that he is impure (Vayikra 13:44).]

What is the meaning of "in our streets"?
It is as if to say,"that we should not have a son or a disciple who
behaves disgracefully in public as did Yeshu the Nazarene."

It is also very important that a parent not show any partiality to one child and thus arouse the jealousy of the other children. The Talmud tell us (Shabbos 10b):

Rabah the son of Mechasiah said in the name of Rav Chama the son of Guriah who said in the name of Rav: "A person should never show favoritism among his children, for the additional two selahs worth of fine cloth that Yaakov gave to Yosef caused Yosef's brothers to grow jealous of him. Events led to other events until, in the end, our forefathers were taken into bondage in Egypt."

Parents must also set a good example for their children. They must be very careful not to make any improper remarks in front of them and certainly not to do anything improper in front of them. They must make every effort to shield their children from all negative influences. Even if the parents themselves sometimes succumb to these influences they must be especially careful not to do so in front of the children. Rather, they should try to condition their children to emulate the pious people, to shun animosity, jealousy, and quarrels.

Moreover, a parent who has been insulted or hit by another person should never tell his child about it, since the child might endanger himself in an attempt to avenge his parent's honor.

There is story told about a pious man who was involved in litigation with someone else. The argument became quite heated, and the pious man's opponent began to heap abuse upon him, accusing him of all sorts of vile things. The pious man's son, who had accompanied his father to the courtroom, became enraged and rose to defend his father.

"Why do you become enraged?" the pious man said to his son. "If my opponent is telling the truth, and I have indeed done these vile things he has accused me of doing, why should you fight with him? I would then be the one who had done wrong, and I would deserve to hear all this abuse. If, however, I am not guilty of these things, why should you pay any attention to the nonsense he speaks? Leave him alone, and let him say whatever he wants. Hashem, before Whom nothing is hidden, knows that my opponent's accusations are false and groundless."

The pious man was at once protecting his son from an unnecessary dispute and teaching him the proper attitude towards life.

In brief, a parent should never hesitate to punish or chastise his child to lead him along the straight path, unless the child has such a wonderful nature that he has no need of it whatsoever.

Chapter Eight

THE REWARDS FOR TEACHING THE TORAH

The rewards for teaching one's child the Torah are very great indeed. The Talmud tells us (Kedushin 30a):

> Rabbi Yehoshua the son of Levi said: "The Scripture considers someone who teaches his child the Torah as if he himself had received it from Mount Sinai. For it is written, And you shall make them known to your sons and the sons of your sons (Devarim 4:9), and immediately thereafter it is written, The day that you stood before God your Lord at Chorev (Devarim 4:10)."
>
> Rabbi Chiya the son of Aba met Rabbi Yehoshua the son of Levi as he was wearing a makeshift head covering and taking his child to the synagogue. He asked him: "Why are you in such a hurry that you could not stop to put on a proper hat?"
>
> Rabbi Yehoshua the son of Levi replied: "Do you find insignificant the importance of teaching Torah to one's children, as implied in the juxtaposition of the two verses, And you shall make them known to your sons (Devarim 4:9) and, The day that you stood before God your Lord at Chorev (Devarim 4:10)?"
>
> After that incident became known, Rabah the son of Rav Huna would not eat even an undercooked scrap of meat before he took his children to the study hall, and Rabbi Chiya the son of Aba would not eat even an undercooked scrap of meat before he read from the Torah with his children and taught them an additional verse.

Although the responsibilty for teaching children the Torah rests primarily with the father, the mother also is rewarded for her efforts in this matter. The Talmud tells us (Berachos 17a; Sotah 21a):

> *Our rabbis have taught: The assurance that the Holy Blessed One gave to women is greater than the assurance He gave to men, as it is written, Arise, you serene women, listen to My Voice, you secure daughters, pay heed to what I say (Yeshayahu 32:9), women being assured serenity and security.*[21]
>
> *Rav said to Rav Ashi: "Since women are not commanded to study the Torah, how do they earn equivalent merit?"*
>
> *He replied: "By taking their children to the synagogues and the study halls and bringing them back from their teachers, and by waiting patiently for their husbands to return from the rabbinical schools."*

> *The Mishnah says: Sometimes a woman may have a form of merit that can suspend retribution for three years...*
>
> *What sort of merit is this? If you say this is the merit of Torah, how does this apply to women who are not commanded to study Torah?*[22]
>
> *...Ravina said: "Indeed, the woman's merit to which the Mishnah refers is the merit of Torah. As to your objection that a woman is not commanded to study the Torah, although she is not commanded to study the Torah she can nevertheless have the merit of Torah. For as a reward for seeing to it that her children study Scripture and Mishnah, and for waiting patiently for her husband to return from the study hall, does she not share equally in their merit?"*

---

21. [Translator's note: Maharsha explains that the period during which Jewish women experienced serenity and security was the one before the Bais Hamikdash was destroyed and the Jews were exiled. Nevertheless, the special consideration given to women during that time is indicative of their special merit in all times.]

22. [Translator's note: The fulfillment of a mitzvah that one has been commanded to do is more meritworthy than the fulfillment of a mitzvah that one has not been commanded to do.]

Now let us look more closely at the nature of these rewards. A child that has been raised to study the Torah brings his parents joy in this world[23] and a share in the world to come.[24] Moreover, one who teaches his children to learn Torah will be rewarded by having the Torah remain with his offspring for always. The Talmud tells us (Bava Metzia 85a):

> *Rabbi Parnach said in the name of Rabbi Yochanan: "If someone is himself a Torah scholar, and his son and grandson are also Torah scholars, the Torah will not depart from his offspring forever, as it is written, And as for Me, this is My Covenant with them, said God, My Spirit that is upon you, and My Words that I have placed in your mouth, they shall not depart from your mouth, and from the mouth of your children, and from the mouth of your children's children, said God, from now until forever (Yeshayahu 59:21)."*
>
> *Rav Yehudah said in the name of Rav: "The Holy Blessed One said: 'I am the Guarantor on this matter.' "*
>
> *What is the meaning of "from now until forever"?*
>
> *Rabbi Yirmiyah said: "From this point on, the Torah always returns to its place of lodging."*
>
> *Rav Yosef fasted one hundred and twenty times.[25] After the first forty fast days he was shown that which is written, They shall not depart from your mouth (Ibid.). After the second forty fast days he was shown that which is written, And from the mouth of your children (Ibid.). After the final forty days he was shown that which is written, And from the mouth of your children's children (Ibid.).*
>
> *Rav Yosef said: "From this point on I need no longer fast, for the Torah always returns to its place of lodging."*

Furthermore, by studying the Torah a son can save his parent

---

23. As it is written, A wise son brings joy to a father (Mishlei 10:1). And it is also written, My son, if your heart is wise my heart shall rejoice as well (Mishlei 23:15).

24. Pesachim 113a.

25. [Translator's note: That the Torah not depart from his children. (Rashi)]

from the judgment of Gehinom.[26] This is implicit in that which is written, Chastise your son and he will relieve you, and he will give delightful things to your soul (Mishlei 29:17). This has been interpreted as saying, "Teach your son the Torah, and he will relieve you from the judgment of Gehinom and usher you into the Garden of Eden with the righteous people." Elsewhere, the Midrash gives an interesting example (Tanchuma, Noach):

> It once happened that Rabbi Akiva was walking in a cemetery and met a blacksmith who was carrying a load of wood on his shoulders and galloping like a horse. Rabbi Akiva commanded that he stop, and he did.
>
> Rabbi Akiva said to him: "My son, why are you doing such difficult work? If you are a bondsman, and your master is laying such a heavy burden on you, I shall redeem you from him and set you free. If you are a poor man I will make you rich."
>
> He replied: "Leave me be, my lord, for I cannot stop."
>
> Rabbi Akiva asked him: "Are you a person or a fiend?"
>
> He replied: "That man died,[27] and every day he is made to gather wood which is then used to burn him."
>
> Rabbi Akiva asked him: "What was your occupation during your lifetime?"
>
> He replied: "I was a tax collector. I was lenient with the rich, and I tormented the poor. What's more, I cahabited with a betrothed maiden on Yom Kippur."
>
> Rabbi Akiva asked him: "My son, did your appointed guards ever tell you that there is a remedy to your situation?"
>
> He replied: "Don't detain me, for the masters of retribution may become furious with me. For that man there is no remedy or redemption. But I did hear them say that if he had a son who would stand amidst the congregation and say, 'Bless the Blessed God,' he would be released from retribution. But that

---

26. [Translator's note: Purgatory.]
27. [Translator's note: An oblique reference to himself.]

man had no son. When he died, his wife was pregnant, and he doesn't know if she gave birth to a son or a daughter. Even if it were a son, who would teach him the Torah?"

Rabbi Akiva asked him: "What is your name?"

He replied: "Arkevasah."

"And the name of your wife?"

He replied: "Shushmirah."

"And the name of your city?"

He replied: "Alduka."

Rabbi Akiva's sympathy was aroused, and he traveled from city to city until he came to that city. He inquired as to the whereabouts of that man's home.

He was told: "May his bones be ground up in Gehinom."

Rabbi Akiva then inquired after the man's wife.

He was told: "May her name and her memory be erased from the world."

Rabbi Akiva then inquired after the man's son.

He was told: "Why, he is still uncircumcized. Not even with the mitzvah of circumcision did his parents concern themselves."

Rabbi Akiva immediately got hold of the son and circumcized him. He sat down with him and started to teach him the Torah, but the boy would not learn.

Rabbi Akiva fasted for forty days until a Divine Echo was heard to ask: "Are you fasting for such a one as this?"

He replied: "Yes."

Only then did the boy begin to learn the alef bais.

Rabbi Akiva took the boy home with him and taught him the Birchas Hamazon blessing after meals, the reading of Shema, and the prayers. He got him to stand up, lead the congregation in prayer, and say, 'Bless the Blessed God.'"

The congregation answered: "Blessed is the Blessed God forever."

At that moment the boy's father was released from retribution. He appeared to Rabbi Akiva in a dream and said to him: "May you have peace of mind, for you have given me peace of mind."

Rabbi Akiva immediately began to recite: "O God, Your

Name lasts forever, Your Remembrance for generation after generation (Tehillim 135:13)."

Elsewhere, the Midrash develops this theme (Midrash Lev Midos):

The protection children provide for their parents is greater than the protection parents provide for their children. Parents can only protect their children, to some degree, from suffering in this world. They imbue their children with life, with strength, and with wealth. When the Day of Judgment comes, however, parents cannot intercede on behalf of their children to save them from the judgment of Gehinom, as it is written, And no one can rescue from My Hand (Devarim 32:39). Avraham could not save Yishmael, nor could Yitzchak save Eisav.

Children, on the other hand, can actually save their parents from the judgment of Gehinom, both grown children and even small children. How? Grown children protect their departed parents by doing good deeds on their behalf. Small children who die young spare their parents the judgment of Gehinom by substituting for it the terrible pain of their loss.

For it is written, Therefore by this shall the guilt of Yaakov be atoned, and this shall be all the fruit that removes his sin (Yeshayahu 27:9). Can fruit remove his sin? Only, this refers to his sons and daughters who are the fruit of his loins.

Rabbi Yehoshua says: "Which measure is greater, the measure for reward or the measure for retribution? I would assume that the measure for reward is greater.[28] Thus, if in the measure for retribution children are dependent on their

---

28. [Translator's note: As the source for this relationship, the Talmud (Sanhedrin 100b) gives that which is written, And He commanded the heavens from above, and He opened the doors of the skies, and He rained down upon them manna to eat... (Tehillim 78:23-24), and that which is written, On this day, all the springs of the great chasm burst, and the windows of the skies were opened (Beraishis 7:11). Rashi explains that the Talmud (Yoma 76a) considers the ratio of windows to doors to be four to one. It is interesting to note that Rashi, in Makos 5b and 23a, brings a different

parents, certainly in the measure for reward parents are dependent on their children to be given the eternal life of the world to come."[29]

And so is it written, And their children shall see it and rejoice (Zechariah 10:7). This comes to teach us that the Holy Blessed One moves fathers and sons close together. If the fathers are sinful and the sons righteous He moves the fathers into the area designated for the righteous people.

And so too is it written, For the one that God loves He chastises, and like a father to a son He reconciles (Mishlei 3:12). In other words, He reconciles the righteous son with the sinful father by bringing them together in the eternal life of the world to come.

Rabbi Chananiah says: "It is written, If a bird's nest appears before you on the way...you shall not take the mother along with the young, surely shall you send away the mother, and the young you can take for yourself (Devarim 22:6-7).

"Is not the mercy of the One through whose Word the world was created greater than the mercy of people? Thus, if people were commanded to show mercy and let the mother go when they take the young, surely it is obvious that when the Holy Blessed One takes the children he will let the parents go free from the judgment of Gehinom."

---

source that results in a relationship of five hundred to one. It is written, For I am God, your Lord, a vengeful Lord who visits the guilt of fathers on sons, onto the third and fourth generations, of My enemies, and who shows kindness to thousands, to those that love Me and keep My commandments (Shemos 20:5-6). The minimum of "thousands" is two thousand, and the ratio of two thousand to four is five hundred to one.]

29. [Translator's note: This means that if children assume responsibility for their parents in the negative sense, certainly they do so in the positive sense as well. If they sometimes die for the sins of their parents, taking the burden of their parents' retribution on their own shoulders, certainly they are capable of providing reward to their parents as well.]

Chapter Nine

THE OBLIGATION TO TEACH OTHERS

The Talmud tells us that whoever teaches Torah to someone else's son is considered to have fathered him (Sanhedrin 19b; 99b):

> Rabbi Yochanan said: "Whoever teaches Torah to the son of another is considered by the Scripture as if he himself had fathered him. For it is written, And these are the generations of Aharon and Moshe (Bamidbar 3:1), but only the names of Aharon's children are mentioned in the following verse, And these are the names of the sons of Aharon... (Bamidbar 3:2). But since Aharon fathered them and Moshe taught them the Torah they are considered the generations of both."

> Rabbi Shimeon the son of Lakish said: "Whoever teaches Torah to someone else's child is considered to have formed him. For it is written, And the people they had formed in Charan (Beraishis 12:5), and Onkelos translates this as the people whom they introduced to the Torah in Charan."

Elsewhere, the Talmud illustrates the importance our sages attached to teaching Torah to the children of others (Bava Metzia 85a):

Rabi[30] *visited the place where Rabbi Elazar the son of Rabbi Shimeon had lived.*

He asked the townspeople: "Did that righteous man leave a son behind?"

They said to him: "Indeed, he had a son. And even harlots who demand four coins in payment gladly pay him eight coins to cohabit with them."[31]

The son of Rabbi Elazar was summoned, and Rabi said to him: "Repent your ways!"

He repented. Rabi ordained him[32] *and sent him to study the Torah with Rabbi Shimeon the son of Isi the son of Lekunia, the brother of his mother. Rabbi Shimeon studied the Torah with him, taught him to wear a rabbinical head covering, and ordained him anew.*

Every day he used to say: "I am returning to my town."

Rabbi Shimeon would answer: "You have been made a Torah scholar, a golden cloth was draped over your head, you are called Rabbi, and still you say, 'I am returning to my town'?"

He replied: "I swear that I shall not say it again."

When he had progressed in his studies, the son of Rabbi Elazar went to study in Rabi's academy. Rabi heard his voice and said: "This voice sounds like the voice of Rabbi Elazar the son of Rabbi Shimeon."

He was told: "It is his son."

Hearing this, Rabi said: "That which is written, The fruit of the righteous are as the living tree (Mishlei 11:30) refers to this Rabbi Yosi, the son of Rabbi Elazar the son of Rabbi Shimeon. And the conclusion of the verse, And who gathers souls is truly wise (Ibid.) refers to Rabbi Shimeon the son of Isi the son of Lekunia."

---

30. [Translator's note: This title is the abbreviated form of Rabbeinu Hakadosh, "our holy master," the Talmudic designation for Rabbi Yehudah the Prince.]

31. Because he was extraordinarily handsome.

32. [Translator's note: Rashi explains that Rabi wanted him to be called Rabbi so that he would be motivated to devote himself to the study of the Torah.]

When Rabbi Yosi the son of Rabbi Elazar the son of Rabbi Shimeon died he was brought to the cavern in which his father was buried. A serpent blocked the entrance.

The people said: "Serpent, serpent, make way and let the son enter to the presence of his father."

The serpent did not budge. The people thought that this was because the father was a greater Torah scholar than the son.

Thereupon, a Divine Echo was heard to say: "It is not because one is a greater Torah scholar than the other. It is because the father suffered the agony of learning Torah in a cave, while the son did not."[33]

Rabi visited the place where Rabbi Tarfon had lived.

He asked the townspeople: "Did that righteous man who used to swear by the life of his children leave a son behind him?"

They said to him: "He left no son, but he left behind a daughter who has a son. And even prostitutes who demand four coins in payment gladly pay him eight coins to cohabit with them."

The son of Rabbi Tarfon was summoned, and Rabi said to him: "If you repent your ways I will give you my daughter in marriage."

Some say that he married her. Others say that he married and divorced her. Yet others say that he did not marry her because he didn't want people to think that he had repented in order to marry her.

Why did Rabi go to such extents to induce Rabbi Tarfon's son to repent?

It can be explained according to that which Rabbi Yehudah said in the name of Rav, or according to another version, which Rabbi Chiya the son of Aba said, or according to another version, which Rabbi Shmuel the son of Nachmeini said in the name of Rabbi Yonasan: "Whoever teaches Torah to the son of another is deemed worthy of a place in the heavenly academy, as it is written,

---

33. During the times of religious persecution, Rabbi Elazar the son of Rabbi Shimeon and his father Rabbi Shimeon the son of Yochai spent thirteen years hidden in a cave and studying the Torah (Shabbos 33a).

Therefore, so said God, if you return, then I will take you back,
you shall stand before Me (Yirmiyahu 15:19). And if someone
teaches Torah to the son of an ignorant man he is deemed worthy of
having the Holy Blessed One cancel His harsh decrees because of
him, as it is written, And if you bring forth the precious from the
worthless you shall be like My Mouth (Ibid.)."

The Talmud goes on to point out the greatness of teaching Torah
to the children of others, both in this world and in the world to come
(Sanhedrin 91b):

Rabbi Yehudah said in the name of Rav: "One who withholds
Torah learning from others is considered to have robbed them of the
legacy of their fathers, as it is written, The Torah which Moshe
commanded us is the heritage of the community of Yaakov
(Devarim 33:4). It is the heritage of the Jewish people dating back
to the six days of creation."

Chana the son of Bizna said in the name of Rabbi Shimeon the
Pious: "If someone withholds Torah learning from others even
fetuses in the wombs of their mothers curse him, as it is written,
One who withholds grain will be cursed by the people (Mishlei
11:26). The Hebrew word used here for people is the one used in
reference to fetuses, as in that which is written, And one people
shall be stronger than the other people (Beraishis 25:23). And the
Hebrew word used here for grain is also used as a metaphor for the
Torah, as in that which is written, Arm yourself with grain lest
He grow angry (Tehillim 2:12)."

Ula the son of Rabbi Yishmael said: "He is perforated like a
sieve.[34]*This follows the alternate meaning of the Hebrew word*
used here for cursed whereby it means perforated, as in that which

---

34. [Translator's note: Maharsha explains that Ula and Abaye base their interpre-
tations on Rav Nachman's statement (Avodah Zarah 35b): "To what can a Torah
scholar be compared? To a bottle of fragrant oil. If it is kept open its aroma is strong."
In other words, if he shares his learning with others he is truly appreciated. Ula and
Abaye are saying that if he does not share his learning it will dissipate and desert
him."]

is written, *And he bored a hole in his door (Melachim II 12:10)."*

Abaye said: "He is perforated like a washerman's drainboard."

And what is the reward of one who does teach Torah to others?

Rav Shashess said: "He is deemed worthy of receiving the blessings promised to Yosef, as the abovementioned verse concludes, *And blessings upon the head of the provider (Mishlei 11:26),* the Hebrew word used here for provider also being used in reference to Yosef in that which is written, *And Yosef was the ruler of the land, he was the provider (Beraishis 42:6)."*

Rav Shashess said: "Whoever teaches the Torah in this world is deemed worthy of teaching it in the world to come as well, as it is written, *And as to the quencher, he too shall continue to quench (Mishlei 11:25)."*

Chapter Ten

MASTER AND DISCIPLE

Someone who teaches students, both older ones and younger ones, should not always resort to corporeal punishment or harsh words to maintain discipline. He should use these methods only occasionally, at other times using threats or cajolery, depending on the situation and the disposition of the students. Nevertheless, he should always make sure that they fear him. Such was the custom with our early sages. The Talmud tells us that Rabbeinu Hakadosh[35] instructed his son Rabban Gamaliel to instill dread in his disciples (Kesubos 103b). The Talmud also tells us that a Torah scholar must feel the bitter taste of bile on his lips when he is sitting before his master (Shabbos 30b).

Elsewhere, the Talmud discusses the relationship between teacher and disciple (Sotah 47a):

> The left hand should always repel while the right hand beckons,[36] not like Elisha who repelled Gaychazi with both hands, and not like Yehoshua the son of Perachiah who repelled Yeshu the Nazarene with both hands.

---

35. See Footnote 30.

36. [Translator's note: This is metaphorically saying that the teacher must not get to close to his disciple, nor too distant from him either.]

What was the incident involving Elisha?

It is written,[37] *And Naaman said, Be so kind and take two talents, and he persisted, and he packed two silver talents in two purses, with two suits of clothing, and he (Gaychazi) gave them to the two youths, and they carried them before him, and he came to the hill, and he took them from their hands, and he secreted them in the house, and he sent away the people and they left, and he came and stood near his master, and Elisha said to him, From where have you come, Gaychazi? and he said, Your servant has not gone here or there, and he said to him, My mind did not wander off when the man turned about from his chariot towards you, is this a time to take silver and to take clothing and olive orchards and vineyards and sheep and cattle and bondsmen and bondswomen? (Melachim II 5:23-26).*

Why did Elisha accuse him of taking eight when, in fact, he only took the silver and the clothing?

Rav Yitzchak said: "At that time Elisha was studying the chapter entitled 'The Eight Vermin'. When Gaychazi appeared Elisha said to him: 'Villain, has the time arrived when you must take eight gifts as a reward for studying the laws pertaining to the eight vermin?'"

Then Elisha said, as the chapter concludes, But let the leprosy of Naaman adhere to you and to your offspring forever, and he went out from before him leprous as snow (Melachim II 5:27).

Afterwards, it is written, And four people were lepers (Melachim II 7:3). Rabbi Yochanan said: "These were Gaychazi and his three sons."

---

37. [Translator's note: The entire chapter describes the events leading up to the confrontation between Elisha and Gaychazi. It tells of Naaman, a great Syrian general, who was a leper. He heard that the prophet Elisha might be able to help him, and after securing the permission of the king of Syria, he travelled to Eretz Yisrael. Elisha cured him of the leprosy but refused to take any of the lavish gifts Naaman tried to give him. After Naaman left to return to Syria, Elisha's servant Gaychazi hurried after him. He told Naaman a spurious tale of two young men who had just come from the mountains of Ephraim and asked him for a talent of silver and two suits of clothing.]

It is written, And Elisha came to Damascus (Melachim II 8:7).

Why did he go?

Rabbi Yochanan says: "He went to convince Gaychazi to return through teshuvah, but Gaychazi did not repent.

"Elisha said to him: 'Repent!'

"He replied: 'This I have learned from you. Whoever sins and causes others to sin is not given the opportunity to repent.'"

What was it that Gaychazi had done?

Some say that he used a magnet to lift Yeravam's golden calf-idol high up into the air.

Others say that he engraved the following verses on the lip of the golden calf-idol: I am God, your Lord (Shemos 20:2). You shall not have any other deities before Me (Shemos 20:3).

Still others say that he turned away the rabbis who came to study with Elisha. For it is written, And the sons of the prophets said to Elisha, Behold now, the place where we sit before you is too cramped for us (Melachim II 6:1), the inference being that until this time there was no crowding.

What was the incident involving Yehoshua the son of Perachiah?

When King Yanai killed the rabbis his sister hid Rabbi Shimeon the son of Shetach.[38] *Yehoshua the son of Perachiah escaped to Alexandria in Egypt.*

When peace returned Rabbi Shimeon the son of Shetach sent him a message: "From me, Yerushalayim, the holy city, to you, Alexandria of Egypt, my sister: My husband is in your midst, and I am devastated."

Yehoshua the son of Perachiah thought: "Apparently, peace has returned."

When he returned he visited a certain inn where he was received with great honor. He was sitting and singing the praises of the lodging place when his disciple Yeshu said to him: "My master,

---

38. [Translator's note: He was her husband.]

the hostess is bleary eyed."

He said: "Villain! Is this with what you busy yourself?"

He called forth four hundred trumpeters, and to their accompaniment, he ostracized Yeshu. Every day Yeshu would come before Yehoshua the son of Perachiah, but he would not release him from his ostracism. One day Yeshu came before him while he was in the middle of reciting the Shema. He considered releasing him, and since he could not interrupt the Shema to speak, he clapped his hands together. Yeshu mistook this as a sign of rejection. He went off and erected a structure and worshipped at it.

Yehoshua the son of Perachiah said to him: "Repent!"

He replied: "This I have learned from you. Whoever sins and causes others to sin is not given the opportunity to repent."

And it was said: Yeshu the Nazarene used sorcery. He instigated the Jewish people and led them astray.

Chapter Eleven

THE TORAH OF SCHOOLCHILDREN

It is the responsibility of every community to provide an adequate number of competent teachers for its children. The Talmud tells us (Bava Basra 21a):

> Rava said: "The proper number of children for one teacher is twenty-five. If there are fifty, two teachers must be hired. If there are forty a platform head[39] is appointed and he is paid by the town."
>
> And Rava also said: "If one teacher of children is learned and there is another teacher who is more learned the first teacher is not dismissed. Why? Because if there will be only one teacher in the town he might become lax."
>
> Rav Dimi from Neharda'a said: "On the contrary, if the first one is dismissed the second one will certainly become even more diligent in his studies, for it has been said: 'Jealousy among scholars proliferates wisdom.'"[40]
>
> And Rava also said: "If there are two teachers, one more learned but less attentive to the children, the other less learned but more attentive, the more learned one is appointed. The children's errors

---

39. An assistant to the teacher who listens to the lesson along with the children and then reviews it with them.

40. [Translator's note: Rashi explains that he will be concerned that the first one will try to embarrass him in front of the townspeople by engaging him in a debate.]

will eventually disappear of their own accord."

Rav Dimi from Neharda'a said: "The one who is more attentive is appointed, because once an error has been absorbed it cannot be eradicated."

For it is written, For six months did Yoav stay there with all Yisrael, until he had destroyed every male in Edom (Melachim I 11:16).

When he came before David, David asked him: "Why did you do this?"

He replied: "Because it is written, I will erase the male of Amalek (Shemos 17:14)."

David said: "You have taken the Hebrew word which means trace and read it with an incorrect pronunciation by which it means male."

Yoav replied: "I was taught that the word is male."

David went to ask Yoav's teacher. He asked: "How is the word read?"

The teacher replied: "The males of Amalek."

David grabbed a spear with the intent to kill him.

Yoav asked: "Why?"

David replied: "Because it is written, Cursed is the one who does the work of God negligently (Yirmiyahu 48:10)."

Yoav said: "Leave the man be, and let him remain with the curse."

He replied: "The verse concludes, And cursed is the one who withholds his sword from blood (Ibid.)."

Some say that he then killed him. Others say he did not.

The children themselves must also be given to understand what they can accomplish with their learning. Thus, they will be encouraged to be diligent in their studies. The Talmud tells us (Shabbos 119b):

Rav Hamnuna said: "Yerushalayim was destroyed because its inhabitants did not provide Torah schools for the children, as it is written, Poured out on the child in the street (Yirmiyahu 6:11). Why was destruction poured out on Yerushalayim? Because the child was in the street."

...Rabbi Shimeon the son of Lakish said in the name of Rabbi Yehudah the Prince: "The world could not exist were it not for the warm breath[41] of schoolchildren."

Rav Pappa said to Abaye: "What of the warm breath of the likes of you and me?"

He replied: "The warm breath of someone who has sinned cannot be compared to the warm breath of those that do not know sin."

And Rabbi Shimeon the son of Lakish also said in the name of Rabbi Yehudah the Prince: "This I have learned from my forefathers: It is forbidden to disturb the Torah study of schoolchildren even for something as important as the rebuilding of the Bais Hamikdash."

And Rabbi Shimeon the son of Lakish also said: "Any town that refuses to establish a Torah school for its children should be destroyed."

Ravina said: "It is excommunicated."

The rewards of Torah teachers who devote themselves to their task for the sake of Heaven are very great indeed. The Talmud tells us (Taanis 24a; Bava Basra 8b):

Rava once decreed a fast day because there was a drought. A man stepped forward to lead the congregation in prayer. As soon as he said, "Who causes the wind to blow," the wind began to blow. As soon as he said, "and causes the rain to fall," the rain began to fall.

Rava asked him: "What is your occupation that you have such merit?"

He replied: "I am a teacher of children. I teach the children of the poor just as I teach the children of the rich, and if someone cannot afford it I take nothing at all. I also have a basket of fish which I use when one of the children neglects his studies.

---

41. [Translator's note: The Torah study.]

It is written, And those that bring righteousness to the many shall be like the stars forever and ever (Daniel 12:3). This refers to the Torah teachers of schoolchildren.

Such as who?

Rav said: "Such that are as devoted as Rav Shmuel the son of Shailas."

Rav once met Rav Shmuel the son of Shailas standing in his garden. He asked him: "Have you abandoned the children who have been entrusted to you?"

Rav Shmuel the son of Shailas replied: "Twelve years have already passed since I last saw this garden, and even now my thoughts are with the children."